Texas Rangers

Interactive Guide to the World of Sports

(Tales of the Texas Rangers and Their Fall and Rise of the Texas Rangers)

Jason Johnston

Published By **Jordan Levy**

Jason Johnston

All Rights Reserved

Texas Rangers: Interactive Guide to the World of Sports (Tales of the Texas Rangers and Their Fall and Rise of the Texas Rangers)

ISBN 978-1-7775767-3-8

No part of this guidebook shall be reproduced in any form without permission in writing from the publisher except in the case of brief quotations embodied in critical articles or reviews.

Legal & Disclaimer

The information contained in this book is not designed to replace or take the place of any form of medicine or professional medical advice. The information in this book has been provided for educational & entertainment purposes only.

The information contained in this book has been compiled from sources deemed reliable, and it is accurate to the best of the Author's knowledge; however, the Author cannot guarantee its accuracy and validity and cannot be held liable for any errors or omissions. Changes are periodically made to this book. You must consult your doctor or get professional medical advice before using any of the suggested remedies, techniques, or information in this book.

Upon using the information contained in this book, you agree to hold harmless the Author from and against any damages, costs, and expenses, including any legal fees potentially resulting from the application of any of the information provided by this guide. This disclaimer applies to any damages or injury caused by the use and application, whether directly or indirectly, of any advice or information presented, whether for breach of contract, tort, negligence, personal injury, criminal intent, or under any other cause of action.

You agree to accept all risks of using the information presented inside this book. You need to consult a professional medical practitioner in order to ensure you are both able and healthy enough to participate in this program.

Table Of Contents

Chapter 1: 20 Simple Tips To Keep In Mind 1

Chapter 2: Practice Tips 13

Chapter 3: Drills And Skills 17

Chapter 4: Common Flaws In Youth Players 31

Chapter 5: Outfield Flaws....................... 43

Chapter 6: Origins & History Quiz Time.. 49

Chapter 7: Jerseys & Numbers 57

Chapter 8: Famous Quotes 66

Chapter 9: Catchy Nicknames 77

Chapter 10: The Ryan Express................ 85

Chapter 11: Statistically Speaking 89

Chapter 12: The Trade Market 99

Chapter 13: Draft Day 109

Chapter 14: Odds & Ends 117

Chapter 15: Outfielders 125

Chapter 16: Infielders 134

Chapter 17: Pitchers & Catchers 144

Chapter 18: World Series 156

Chapter 19: Heated Rivalries................ 166

Chapter 20: The Awards Section 173

Chapter 21: The American Dream City . 177

Chapter 22: Young At Heart 181

Chapter 1: 20 Simple Tips To Keep In Mind

1. be gentle with the athletes. It only takes some seconds to rip an individual's confidence and it will take several weeks to rebuild it back up. Therefore, instead of retelling them their mistakes and then reaffirm the actions they were able to do right, and alert them to mistakes they made. Let them breathe and develop the game in their own way. It is impossible to emphasize the importance of this. We all know about the stereotypical "little league dad," however, while many parents claim they'll never let it occur, but it happens. In addition, in this day and age the game is supposed to be enjoyable. If your players aren't enjoying themselves, they're never likely to be motivated to play baseball at all in the first place. As a coach, or as a parent, you must always be reminding players that they're there for fun, not be concerned about instant outcomes. Reminding your players to relax

and clearly demonstrating to them that you're always happy with your actions helps them to enjoy their time playing, and builds confidence in themselves. There is nothing more satisfying than having your parent or coach affirm that they are happy for you.

2. Conduct a parent-teacher gathering at the start of the season prior to the start of the season. As someone who has been personally involved in an organization for little leagues which had more than 400 players I am aware that parents are very mad! Be assured you don't want to argue with irrational kids league parents about an issue which could easily been avoided. Explain all the rules and guidelines you've put in place as a coach. It will help keep any confusion from possibly arise later on. It could also make the difference between angry parents of the little league shouting at you! This, as we all know regardless of the prevention actions taken, it is an extremely high chance in coaching young baseball. This is just the territory, so prepare.

3. Do not, in any way be a fan of any team. Many coaches say they don't never played a game of favorite, but it is that it is the truth. Other players are likely to recognize the issue and be disenchanted rapidly. At any level of baseball up to professional level there is a significant political aspect in baseball, and you shouldn't be caught in the trap of offering some players special benefits. Even though it can be hard to break your friend's son's heart, if you give him his starting position at shortstop to a different player than him but it's likely to blow over and be beneficial to the team. It's an ideal opportunity for parents to get in problems. Instruct them that the players who are qualified to play are going to play, and everyone is given the opportunity to show their worth.

4. Do not over-coach. This is a point I cannot stress enough. Everyone hates a coach who keeps a constant eye on everyone. Allow the children to play at this stage, again, the sport is intended to be fun and not a chore. Let the kids make mistakes, and take lessons from

their mistakes. Be assured that they'll recognize when they've done something wrong, and screaming down their throats will not solve any issue. In fact they could actually make the issue more difficult. There is however the right time and place for a thorough investigation involved in a player's case. As an example, a person who's behavior is erratic or making mistakes in their thinking is a problem that needs to be dealt with since they're easily fixable. A player discourteous and is adamant in his responses to coaches is another issue that needs to be addressed in a timely manner to resolve the problem. There's no room for in the game for disrespectful and non-adherent players. If a player does get out of line, others will see quickly and you'll have to relinquish control of your group. In the event that you intend to win games, losing the control of the players in your team is not the recipe for success.

5. You must be confident about yourself as coach. Children are sponges and they pick up even the smallest changes in tone, mood, or

tone. In the case of example, if you're not sure about your play-call to a pinch-hitter or steal call, they'll notice it immediately. Every action you take as a coach must be confident. If you are speaking to your players, do it confidently. Make sure they know that you're the one in charge, and that neither parent nor participant will be able influence your decisions. In particular, with the parents inform them early throughout the season that you're the head coach and that you won't get influenced by their complaints. It's your job to be the boss. Communicate the message to parents and the players.

6. You should find an assistant coach, perhaps two. It is extremely challenging to have one person manage an entire group of children aged 12-15 and is almost impossible. Therefore, you should find an assistant coach, or even two. The addition of an extra pair of eyes is never a bad thing particularly when you're dealing with children who play with at baseballs and bats. This will not only aid you in the teaching however, it can also aid you

with dangers that might arise their own. There is nothing more painful than a child of 10 using an aluminum bat to the forehead. The additional coaches can assist you to conduct effective training sessions as well. You could, for instance, employ one coach to focus on hitting the cage while a different coach assists the infielders, and the final coach has an in-game bullpen for your catchers and pitchers.

7. Your role as a model is important. No matter if you'd like to play the role of an example for your team members are bound admire your example. If you're always arguing with the umpires, and ignoring other teams and your team's players will come be influenced to think that they could perform the same. Be positive and have a positive mental attitude all the time. Positive attitudes are infectious, so is yours something you should be watching? Also, dress in a code you are able to hold yourself to. Do not show up wearing cutoff tops and jeans that are ripped.

Make yourself look like a professional and act in the manner of a coach.

8. Every player must be treated equally regardless of their level of expertise. This is in line when playing the favorites. Everyone should be given the same amount of time and guidance. However, it is true that the ones who aren't as talented will receive less training, but that's an entirely separate topic for discussion. According to the saying "you're only the best as your weakest player'. Therefore, you should make sure you coach your weakest player to the point where he's as great than the rest!

9. Avoid playing the blame game. In the aftermath of a loss you shouldn't be blaming anyone. It's not the fault of the umpire as well as the fault of the person who kicked the ball into the ground to let scoring the winner. Your team's fault and not the fault of a specific person. If you lose as a group, then you're losing together. Instead, you should focus on winning the game and the proper

preparation to prepare for the game. You can also discuss what that your team should do to prepare for the following game, and also the things that the potential to be improved. Be careful not to inappropriately single someone for a particular reason. In the past, for instance, I talked about the person who made a mistake in allowing the winning team to score. Therefore, instead of saying "we need to field ground balls better.", what if you said "As a team our defense was a little rusty tonight, we will work on it at practice for the next game" or similar to that to make sure that players don't feel they're on the losing side of their shoulders.

10. Learn the difference between physical and mental errors. They are two completely distinct things that must be dealt with in separate ways. An error in physical form, throwing the fly ball throwing them off, throwing a poor throw and so on. should be dealt in a manner that is accompanied by comfort. It's not like the player made an error with intention, therefore comfort the player

by saying, "you'll get it next time." Or "everybody misses a few." The truth is that screaming or yelling at the person can only cause him to play more tightly and stress the situation. But a mistake made by a mind should be handled by sterner means. This does not refer to yelling at a player or making him a target of teammates. You should wait until the time of the inning is right with the inning and then take him towards the side, and then remind the player that his mental mistakes are totally avoidable, and the player must "keep his head in the game." Any action which conveys that mental mistakes are primarily result of a lack of focus or negligence.

11. Coaches are not player. It was the time to play an athletic. It's for youngsters, not you. It's true that a majority of coaches in the little league tend to be enticed by the thought of reliving their glory days in high school during their time as coaches and players. Do not become "that guy." Your role as a coach must include promoting the joy of playing baseball

to the kids, and, above all else is to let the children be having fun! While you're in the business of promoting your sport and having fun, but your aim is to assist children develop as individuals. They should be taught a lesson they'll take with them throughout their adult life. Coaches from colleges say that there's no more satisfying satisfaction than watching a player who they had coached at college be able to come back 10-15 years later and claim that the lessons they learned will be helpful in their adult lives. This doesn't just happen for players at the top levels of baseball, either. It's never too late to assist the child develop strategies that they'll employ throughout the rest of their life.

12. Take responsibility. If you've made a poor choice that cost your squad the match, do not be scared to admit the situation. Your players know that it wasn't your fault. If you are held accountable for your actions, they'll be able to respect you and admire your character even more. What's the most damaging thing result of acknowledging your error? It really

will be a simple little playing game. The idea is to have entertaining, and it's certainly unlikely that you'll lose your job.

13. Be a part of your teammates. One of the best teachers I ever had was while I played 14u in travel ball. He was a pro and also a Division 1 athlete which meant that his experience was extensive and he had lots of wisdom to transmit to us youngsters. In my opinion, the thing that was what made him an excellent coach instead of just a typical run of the mill teacher was his capacity to at the appropriate moments, be fun and bond with his students. This made us feel like he was a part of us and made us feel like a team. However, this wasn't always the case all the time because he did an excellent job of setting a clear line to ensure where he still was the coach we had and would not shy away from coaching and disciplining us in the event that the situation got out of hand. It's important to not be afraid to talk and be a fun person with your team members, but be careful not to get to the point in which they

don't be able to listen due to the fact that they perceive you to be the only one.

Chapter 2: Practice Tips

What is the best way to conduct an EFFECTIVE and EFFICIENT exercise

1. Practice Times- Arrival and Departure.

a. Establish times for both, and adhere to the set times. The arriving time will determine what is most effective for you as a coach. However, make sure that you're always at the correct time. This is a way to be your role model to your teammates. Being late to coaches look terrible, and if you consistently arrive promptly on time you will be a role model for your kids. Parents put in an effort to be more accountable and get the kids arriving in time.

b. Set your practice's close time fixed and do the best you can to not surpass the time limit. As coaches, you're working with children, and over-killing practices can only bore youngsters and irritate parents. But, putting off practice often is a great technique to implement as an incentive program. "If everyone gives a 100% for the last drill we can end 20 minutes early!"

It is possible to observe a significant transformation in the mind as well as attitude and work. However, don't use this method as a means to skip the practice, and create more time for you. It won't work since the time you finish early need to be prepared with your children's parents who have picked them up from the initial ending time.

2. Utilize your time effectively.

Do not waste time performing ineffective and often unproductive practice exercises. One of the best methods to ensure that your team is engaged is to ensure that all members are actively engaged throughout the day. If you are teaching drills and are requiring kids to wait for five minutes in between turns, the practice is likely to take an unforgiving turn. The situation will turn into the worst, as you've now losing the attention of your players, which means they'll now be doing anything to entertain themselves which can result in disruption to your training as well as wasting your time. Therefore, keep them engaged. do not forget that you're working children with tiny attention to attention spans. The most effective method to beat boredom, in my view using a rotating system with multiple stations. Split your group into groups based on the position, and give the members a set period of time at every station. It will ensure that they are actively engaged throughout the time.

3. Make a Practice Schedule.

If you're planning to watch an Major League game, go early in order to observe their games' pregame preparations. Every single thing they perform is timed through to the second. That's why they're very successful in keeping everything on time and well-organized. It is evident that we're working with kids and not experienced major leaguers, but this concept is applicable to both. This can help your team keep their attention and be entertained throughout practice. Therefore, at least a couple of days prior to each practice, take a seat and write down the plans for every one. Perhaps you can dedicate a notebook or file on your computer for practice schedules. This can help you be aware of and recall the drills you have already practiced, etc.

Example practice plan:

5:15-5.30 - Arrive, Stretch, Warm up

5:30-6:30 - Station rotations

Group 1	Group 2	Group 3	Time
Hitting	Fielding	Pitching	5:30-5:50
Fielding	Pitching	Hitting	5:50-6:10
Pitching	Hitting	Fielding	6:10-6:30

6:30-6:45- Live scenarios

6:45-7:00- Fun game. (Incentive reward)

Chapter 3: Drills And Skills

Infield

1. Bare Hand Shuffles / Tosses In the beginning of every infield practice, I believe that a fundamental warm-up drill is essential. It is so because, as pitchers need to loosen their arms relaxed when they are in the bullpen for pitching, fielders have to get warm hands as well. This is the ideal solution. Make infielders team up, and take off their gloves. Then, space them out about 6-8 feet. Make sure that players are in a proper playing position. If feet are slightly larger than shoulders, left hand inches ahead of the right. The players butts must be at a low level with hands spread.

When players have found the correct place, they should shuffle balls while tossing and catching balls using your left hands (right hand is for righties). Tosses should have a slight angle and students should be practicing throwing balls using soft hands. Tell players to imagine the ball in terms of an egg, and then take it in very gentle. This exercise helps develop hand eye coordination, and helps in hitting balls with gentle hands. This is an essential tool in players in the field. It can be made to work with shorter hops like forward and backhands.

2. Power Infield (Mass Fungo)Power Infield utilized all across the country across all levels

of baseball and is among the most efficient and effective exercises that can be found. Power infield is a method which aims to get many repetitions which in baseball is arguably more crucial than any other aspect. Then, assign your players into their spots, and ideally two players per place. The drill is a requirement for two coaches, too. Each coach selects two spots in the infield to strike ground balls twice. Most commonly, the one coach hits shortstop and first base. The other strikes to second and third base. There is a myriad of ways to approach this using different coaches hitting various players, and even throwing. No matter how the power drill is executed, it could be among the most efficient exercises you can use.

3. The short Hop and Throw is an excellent way to improve your infielder's fielding positions and getting the ball in their belt before setting the feet in order to execute a precise throw at the target base. Make sure that your players take a proper posture for the field as illustrated above. They can then

shuffle or skip their ground ball one time. It is crucial to not throw the ball, and avoid throwing the ball at an angle that is downwards or even spike the ball. Spiking it creates an impossible situation for motion of the ball upon the ground or in dirt. Don't make the mistake of hopping one time towards the player, and ensure that he is able to strike the ball by funneling it through his belt before placing his feet in the direction of the object he's throwing to. Make sure that you never allow your players in the field to take the same "crow hop" as your outfielders might. Instead, make sure they're instead taking a shuffle step using their feet. As an example, your feet need to be left to right and after which you throw them to the side and then take your rear foot (right foot) to the left of your foot.

Outfield

1. This is known as the Quarterback Drill- This drill is considered to be one of the most well-known drills for outfield in practice, yet it may

certainly be among the top. The drill that is simple and easy to learn is utilized by professional players in the present. The drill is referred to as the "quarterback drill' due to its simplicity, as it's similar to the quarterback who throws to wide receivers. Start your outfielder at a distance of 10 feet from you and have both feet pointed towards you. This is being the "quarterback." Use the option "drop step and go," and make sure to point towards the direction you would like your athlete to move. The drill, just like power infield, is about repetition.

Training makes perfect, so don't be scared to invest a lot of time in basic drills such as this as well as power infield. Be sure your the players use the drop step prior to beginning with the pursuit of fly balls. Drop steps are the moment when players drop their hips in direction towards the ball, instead of turning around in a full circle. Be sure to ensure that players are following efficient and swift routes towards the ball. The most efficient way to get towards the ball one where the ball player has to travel less ground in order to get to the location, which is likely, the straightest path to the ball. A key aspect of coaching this exercise is to never permit players to "drift" to the spot in which they'll be able to catch the ball. Instruct them to give 100 percent to arrive at the area and then try their best to arrive early so that they can have time to get set up and then catch the fly ball.

2. Tennis Racquet Balls- If you find an older tennis racquet lying about and have a few tennis balls, it is the perfect way to aid youngsters develop the ability to hit sky flying balls with no being afraid of hitting the face with a typical baseball. It's a great drill since young players are often scared of ball hitting

them which is why there's any better way to assist them to overcome their anxiety. In terms of the exercise goes, it's quite simple. Set your players on the outfield and throw the ball the highest you are able!

3.The Crow Hop- Every young player in the outfield must learn how to crow hop! Crow hops are the motion that allows players to make use of all their momentum and power to create an effective throw towards the base they want. The ability of outfielders to crow hop is crucial as players get older and start to strike the ball into outfields more often, which results in more throws coming from the outfield, resulting in close play on bases. Encourage your players to strike the ball when there's a possibility of play. They should then throw the ball in front with their left. When they are transferring the ball into their throwing hand, start to move the back foot in front of the front foot. They can use the foot that is behind to pull away to provide the force required to throw the ball with force into the bag. The image below will help to

provide more information.

4. Communication Drills are an integral aspect of playing in the outfield is to be able to converse with your two outfielders and your players in the field. Be sure to train the players you want to have prioritization in these scenarios. The centerfielder is responsible for all outfielders, along with all infielders. The corner outfielders are responsible for the infielders. Set your players in their spots and then hit the fly ball in "no mans land" or the "grey area." These are the outfield positions where batted balls are often able to drop into. Your fielders must communicate who is to be responsible for

catching the ball with voice. Only the person shouting something should be the one who is aiming to catch the ball. An acceptable method to use for the baseball to be caught include yelling, "mine, mine," or "ball, ball, ball" and so on. It is important to practice this since proper communication can to avoid serious injuries.

Pitching

1. Flat Grounds: Flat ground can be a fantastic way for pitchers of every age to practise and develop their mechanics and pitches. To practice flat ground, let your pitchers pair up, and spread out within the range they typically pitch from. Flat ground isn't meant to be a maximum effort training exercise. It's intended to be focused on smaller aspects of control and mechanics rather than throwing the ball in the most forceful way you can as many youth pitchers practice. Let the pitchers play the sequence you want them to go through. As an example, ask them to throw 4 seams, 4 two seams, 4 shifts at the end of the

wind-up. They can also throw out of the stretch, too. When you observe this drill be sure to keep an eye on the pitcher's technique.

2. Balance Point Drill participants to complete the exercise of balance let them do the regular wind-up routine. But, once they've come to the balance point, have them stop and remain there for up to 3 minutes. As they are holding it, the coach must be looking at their body posture and ensure that everything is properly aligned. It is also possible to add variants to the drill, using things like, at the point they are at their equilibrium place, they should take the ball and then touch the rubber 3 times at a slow pace. All the while keeping your balance can be difficult. This exercise also instructs players not to hurry through their pitch.

3. The Towel Drill: The towel drill is one of the things I was taught growing as a child. I think it's very unconventional and most people aren't aware of. But, it is highly beneficial because it helps to develop the various mechanics of good techniques, such as reaching toward your home plate. Get some dishtowels from the past that have lost any usage. Take some athletic tape and then tape the towel to the middle and almost creating an elongated handle middle. Leave the edges of the towel to each side taped and untaped. The coach should stand on the mound, holding the glove. The goal of the exercise is to get the young pitcher to reach for and take the end of a towel from the glove. Be sure

that the instructor is sufficiently far away that the player actually has to reach out and extend towards their goal.

Catching

1. Receiving - Being a catcher is about the way you take in (catch) the ball. If the catcher is able to catch strikes that appear like balls as he struggles to take the ball in his hands, and you're in an issue. If you could help a catcher take balls to create them to look like strikes, you're in a position to gain a significant benefit. This method is known as framing but it is a far more complex subject to master. A catcher should be able of receiving the ball by

using a firm wrist as well as soft hands. If you've ever watched an important game in the major leagues take note of how, when the catcher receives the ball he does not allow the ball to affect his arm, as his wrist is essentially still. An excellent exercise for this type of exercise is to perform a hand-free practice of receiving. Don't use gloves for this exercise. The catcher sits down in a regular receiving position. The player is 10-15 feet from the coach's catch position. The coach starts with a backhand throw to the strike zone that is imagined. The catcher must develop soft hands as well as firmly securing the ball in a similar manner as we discussed earlier. While you work, increase velocity until you're throwing the ball at a rapid pace.

2.Blocking Practices - Every successful player must be able to block and do it well to be able to block well. One of the best drills to master how blocking is to begin without a ball. Begin in the squat of your catcher and then drop into the proper blocking position. An ideal blocking position is comprised of some things.

A. Falling down until your knees, putting your glove the space between your legs.

B. You have your other hand hidden behind the glove.

C. Your chest must be reversed while your head is down.

The purpose of blocking is to stop the ball using your chest. You should also keep your chest turned inwards, which can prevent the ball from rolling around.

Chapter 4: Common Flaws In Youth Players

Hitting Flaws

1. The Bat is being held incorrectly Players should keep both hands in one hand using their second set of knuckles in a straight line. The players should be taught to keep the bat at the tips of their fingers and not firmly set into their hands, as this can accelerate the whipping of bats and increase speed.

2. Uncorrected stances - For younger athletes, it's recommended to keep their feet aligned when at their batting stance. Certain players prefer to place their front foot in the back foot. This is known as an open posture. Certain players also use closed stance. At this stage, it's an excellent practice to train the players to take a balanced position. I ensure that I inform my students prior to each single rep to examine their feet. When they've heard me tell them the same thing a hundred times, they will eventually learn independently and begin to examine their

feet on their own until they get at which they no longer need to do any checking in any way.

3. Inability not to "Squash the Bug"- As a coach for young baseball players through the winter months and into the beginning of spring, one the biggest mistakes that I find in their swing mechanics is the inability to utilize the lower part of their body during their swing. In other words, they are not able the need to "squash the bug." This is what I refer to as and others refer to it as squashing bugs because youngsters can connect to the concept better than they could say "rotate your back foot so your hips get through the ball." This is among the most important things I look for in youth players.

4. Slow or Long Swings- Some signs of a hitter with an extended swing are being slowed down a lot and rolling ground balls that are to their pulling side, or failing to catch the speed of fastballs. Long swing means the hand of the hitter is drifting away from the baseball, instead of straight towards the ball. A player

who takes a short swing has hands that remain within his body. If a hitter has a lengthy swing will have hands that quickly leave his body. The best way to correct this issue is to practice one-handed training exercises with a focus on directing the handle of the bat towards the ball.

5. Inappropriate or unneeded movement - A large number youngsters today are watching MLB games and although a number of items they watch on television can be useful to understand but some aren't. The things they do while hitting such as massive leg kicks, big hits and upper cuts that are used by MLBs top sluggers, aren't items we'd like our kids as well as children to learn upon. This kind of style of hitting should not be tried until the players have grown older and know the nuances of what they're doing. The styles that are used at the young or little league level might be considered an unnecessary movement. Every wasted movement in the swing of a child creates a harder time hitting the baseball than it is already. If you, as a

coach notice your kids doing to do these things, make them aware that simpler is better, and remain with the fundamentals. If they stay with basic bread-and-butter principles they'll be much more effective.

6. Do not walk straight/ "Stepping in the Bucket"Have you ever seen a child take a swing only to have his head forward shoulder, and front foot flutter out of the way away from home plate? It could be a sign of the old cliche "stepping in the bucket." This happens the case when a player instead of striking straight at the pitcher, he turns away from the plate, which causes his shoulder and leg to open up and, in doing so, moves his head off the ball. The hitter with this problem, unless it is fixed, will continue be struggling to hit the ball. It's very difficult to hit something that you cannot be able to see. If you're stepping into the bucket and removing your head away from the ball, there is no way to tell. The best way to address this is by lining the batter on something. Make sure that they finish their steps with the same line they

started with. In this case, place both feet in the inner area of the batter's box while practicing. Toss them a ball to throw and then see which side of their feet ends upwards. Make them look to observe where the ball is as well. If the ball fell off of the ground behind them, ensure that you point it towards them, and then encourage them to walk straight towards the ball as well as the pitcher. Another fantastic solution is by using a two-by-four plank. Make them stand on the two-by-four, trying to stay on the floor and remain steady all at all the time. The player will be forced to move directly toward the pitcher and ball while also working to maintain their balance on the plate.

7. Incorrectly Loading Hands or Not Loading properly- Loading your hands properly as an a player is crucial. It creates momentum that drives toward the ball. The most effective way to define the process is through what they refer to as"the rubber band effect. As if hitters had the rubber band between their hands as well as their front foot. If they put

their hands inwards toward their shoulders and then walk with their feet in in the opposite direction to the pitcher the rubber band will build the elastic energy. When the player is able to swing, and then begins to move their hands to the front the energy stored is discharged onto the baseball. This is why it's important to taking your hands off. The players who don't take their hands off are missing the entire benefit. The most effective way to practice loading your hands is to do teework. Players should cut multiple times off of the Tee. Every time you are causing the batter to fill their hands, let them increase the load when it is necessary.

A. The image taken by Triple Crown winner Miguel Cabrera illustrates the effect of rubber bands clearly. The lines drawn between his front and hands expands (changing between red and yellow) leading to energy building before being let off onto the ball when Miguel begins to let his hands go to the ball.

8. The Front Foot is Down late Baseball players who hit consistently with a lot of force, regardless of in the event that they are not out they always keep their timing right. The timing of the front foot (striding) precisely at the right time is among the most important factors in hitting. In the event that your front foot isn't walking and descending in time, a hitter struggles to keep pace with the ball. This was a problem I had to deal with as a child. I was able to interact with kids of higher age in my teens. I had never played against pitching with the same velocity as I now saw. I always slowed down on their fastballs, and I was unable to determine the reason. I was observing the ball very well and was thinking that I ought to be over the ball. My front foot wasn't moving on time and it was causing all other parts of my swing to be

lagging in the background, resulting in me getting late with fastballs. The only method to solve this issue is to get the batter to put in an effort to keep their feet down in time. The best rule of thumb for coaches to teach players to put their front foot in when the arm of the pitcher reaches the letter "L" during his release point. But, every player will have an individual timing mechanism, and the timing of front foot movements will be different for each player.

9. A bad pitch selection is common. youngsters who are placed in a team that is new or in a stress situation become very nervous. As they get anxious, they are desperate to take an earful so badly that they get so excited and start to hit bad pitches. The reason is that people who are in a slump can cause their depression to become worse as they're eager to come out of their slump and then begin swinging at poor pitches. If you are a baseball player and swing at pitches that are not good typically, you will be thrown out. Help players who swing at poor pitches to lay

back while letting the ball move in the reverse direction. This gives them to have a more time duration to assess whether the pitch is suitable pitch to hit. As a result, they'll hit more high-quality pitches that are suitable to strike.

10. Don't Swing All the Way through the BallIt's hard to tell how many times I've witnessed this type of thing. In the event that a player in youth makes contact with the ball,, he reduces or stop swinging. Power loss if in not following through is a huge loss. One of the best ways to fix the common error is to simply the tee and repeated. When you are watching your batter swing off the tee, you must constantly remind them to complete the swing.

Infield Flaws

1. Refraining from attacking the baseballIt is a huge issue that affects fielders of every level of baseball. Particularly for those with an above average arm since they are convinced they can cover the loss of time through a solid

throwing across the field. The baseball's lack of attack could cause a variety of problems. By not attacking the ball, the ball to go through the ground more quickly and, in turn, gives the ball greater chance to make an errand. The other issue is that the player isn't able to build up enough momentum to throw the ball to the first base, resulting in greater throws that are not correct that if the fielder would had charged the ball. One great way to tackle the issue is what called"the "banana curve" drill. In order to perform the drill, put the obstacle ahead of the infielder and then place the ground balls just ahead of the obstruction. In this way, the player has to move across the obstacle and around the ball, while transferring momentum toward first base. This should lead to the infielder navigating around the baseball, which will result in an "banana" shape.

2. Incorrectly following your throw Another problem with youth players who cause incorrect throws is that they fail to adhere to their throws. I've seen it time and time

repeatedly. A player will attack the ball well then field it, throw and immediately stop their feet. Benefits of following through with your throw is that the quantity of errors that a thrower is able to avoid drastically because they're transferring momentum toward the target. If you can keep your feet in motion, and keeping your body centered on his goal, resulting in an in line throw, too. People often throw in an area while their body is moving to an opposite direction.

3. Working with gloves; Starting instead of down- New players in the field tend to attempt to be in their proper fielding positions and to switch their gloves down in order to play the ball until the end of every second. Problem with this is that it is extremely difficult to adapt to an unplanned leap. It's always simpler for fielders to begin with their hands down, then take a ball towards the chest, and then keep it on their feet rather than try to alter to a new hop and then have the ball slide through their legs. Therefore, as a rule practice, always tell your

fielders to get the gloves on and gradually begin to work their way up to an unnatural step.

Chapter 5: Outfield Flaws

1. The Ball is being caught with one Hand
Young outfielders attempt to accomplish this every single time. You can get under a ball, try to catch it with just one hand, instead of two and voila. The ball is thrown away. The young players, no regardless of how skilled they may be at their age must be instructed to grasp the ball using two hands. Doing this increases their chances of getting the ball caught significantly higher. The use of two hands reduces chances of the ball hitting the glove or palm, and failing to capture the ball.

2. Incompletely understanding the scenario
When you are a position player on the field, it's essential to be aware of the scenario before hitting the ball. It is important for players to collect as much data about what they should do when the ball is struck. In the case of an errant runner at third base with one out, the outfielder must be aware upon a flyball, they need to be in the field and throwing the ball with force at home plate, hoping to knock the runner off in the third

base area. Infielders who do not know about this situation are not to be blamed other than their own ignorance as there is nothing they can do to fix this aside from being more aware and involved in the game.

3.Poor Communication- A lack of communication between outfielders could cause serious collisions that can result in injuries. In the outfield, players should be aware of the need to ask for the baseball. Many youths forget to perform this task because they are concentrated on the task of catching the ball. When practicing, remind players that every time a fly ball is hit, they must ask to the ball. Train them in this ability into their brains until they are able to perform it naturally. If your children are able to call to the ball can help a child avoid a severe accident.

4. The First Step - Outfielders from all ages appear to commit this error. After the ball has been hit, the first time, they begin to walk toward the infield instead of then taking their

first step to the back. This flaw is particularly apparent in line drives that are hard hit. The reason is that at the time you've taken an unintentional step and realize that the ball was hit with force, the ball is over the top of your head and burning. If the person had taken the correct move back immediately, they could have be able to lessen the injury or perhaps even drive the ball away.

5. calling/catching ball at the highest PointThe majority of players do not call or catch the ball from its top level. What I'm referring to is that they must signal and announce the ball while it's the highest. This will give players time to determine who is most likely to play the most effective with the ball. This also prevents players calling for ball and failing to get the ball. The ball should be caught at the highest level simply implies to grab the ball using arms extended, and with a hand that is not gloved beside the ball.

A. The ball being caught in its most elevated position keeps the ball always in your vision. If you catch the ball using a bent arm or even inside your body as many infielders needs you to keep an eyes off the ball for only a short moment, which can lead to an infraction.

Pitching Flaws

1.Not picking up the TargetPitching isn't an easy job at all. Any additional complications is best prevented at all cost. One of the biggest problems with youth pitchers is that they fail to keep eyes on their target. The young pitchers are more likely to glance down, and try to catch the target of the catcher late during their pitch, causing them to be unable to hit their target by larger distances that they're competent of. It is important for coaches to make pitchers keep their eyes on the glove of the catcher for all of their delivery. Equally important is that catchers provide the ball to a lower target in order that they can reach their target, they have a lower chance that the opponent will hit the ball with a sharp angle.

2.Not Following Through/Overthrowing- Pitchers of all ages often try to throw the ball as hard as they possibly can. Although velocity is astonishing, it is often the reason why pitchers are overthrowing. The signs of overthrowing are usually by the fact that the pitcher has been consistently not hitting the strike zone at a high. When they do this, there's an increased chance that they are not doing their job correctly. If they overthrow or do not follow through, it could be very harmful for a child's arm as they're not making use of their upper and lower body in order to hit the ball. This puts a greater volume of stress to the ligaments and tendons of the elbow and shoulder. The pitchers who overthrowing need to be instructed to ease their shoulders and grab the glove of the catcher. In addition, focus on throwing strikes instead of throwing the ball with a lot of force. You should ensure that the player is finishing the delivery completely extended and with their front leg bent and not straight.

3.Throwing Across the Body- This can be a relatively simple problem to identify and rectify. Throwing across your body typically caused by a pitcher's forward foot landing too very far to third base in the case of a right-handed pitcher or first base for lefties, when they have completed their stride. When throwing across your body as well as not keeping the ball in place it, could result in damage to an arm that is young due to the increased amount of strain on the tendons and ligaments of their arm. One way to address this issue is to ask the player draw a line to the left of the middle rubber. Try to get them to aim their front foot in the line as they walk. The body will remain aligned with the the home plate. This will stop them from throwing their bodies.

Chapter 6: Origins & History Quiz Time

1. What was those Texas Rangers known as before they were relocated to Arlington?

a. Montreal Expos

b. Washington Senators

c. Dallas Cowboys

d. Dallas Senators

2. Which year was it that the franchise relocate from Texas to Texas?

a. 1952

b. 1962

c. 1972

d. 1982

3. The Rangers are expected to move into Globe Life Field in 2020. The team has been playing in Globe Life Park since 1994.

a. True

b. False

4. What division are the Texas Rangers currently play in?

a.American League West

b.American League Central

c.National League West

d.National League Central

5. What did the name mean for the stadium where the Rangers played at from 1972 to 1993?

a.AT&T Stadium

b.RFK Stadium

c.Arlington Stadium

d.Griffith Stadium

6. In 1989 in 1989, the Texas Rangers were sold to an investment firm led by whom previous U.S. president?

a.Barack Obama

b.Bill Clinton

c. George H.W. Bush

d. George Bush. Bush

7. The Rangers Mascot, which is named Captain is exactly what species of animal?

a. Cow

b. Bull

c. Horse

d. Lizard

8. Who's the manager with the longest tenure of all time in Texas Rangers history (as of the close of the season in 2019)?

a. Ron Washington

b. Buck Showalter

c. Bobby Valentine

d. A and C

9. What's the name of this team? Texas Rangers' Triple-A team and, if so, where are they in the city of Houston?

a. Fresno Grizzlies

b. Nashville Sounds

c. Toledo Mud Hens

d. Columbus Clippers

10. What was Rangers manager before they relocated to Arlington and then became they the Texas Rangers?

a. Ted Williams

b. Billy Martin

c. Don Zimmer

d. Johnny Oates

11. The Rangers General Manager currently, Jon Daniels, was the youngest manager ever at time to ever be employed in MLB when he was hired in the time of his appointment in 2005, when he was just age 28.

a. True

b. False

12. What is the origin of Texas Rangers' name originate?

a. Walker Texas Ranger TV show

b. An an ode to Old West cowboys

c. The famed police department of the identical name

d. The Dallas Cowboys were formerly the Texas Rangers.

13. What is the number of appearances that The Texas Rangers made in the MLB playoffs (as at the close of 2019's season)?

a. 7

b. 8

c. 9

d. 10

14. In what year was the current edition of the Washington Senators established?

a. 1941

b.1951

c.1961

d.1971

15. This Washington Senators franchise was an expansion team. They are the Minnesota Twins were the original Washington Senators and hold all of their records from the beginning.

a.True

b.False

16. The Washington Senators were a member of what division?

a.American League East

b.National League East

c.American League West

d.National League West

17. What ex- Rangers player has become an expert in color on TV to commentate on Rangers coverage in Fox Sports Southwest?

a. Charlie Hough

b. Kenny Rogers

c. Nolan Ryan

d. C.J. Nitkowski

18. What number of World Series did the Washington Senators take home?

a. 0

b. 1

c. 2

d. 3

19. Who was the initial manager of the franchise that was it was the Washington Senators?

a. Eddie Yost

b. Jim Lemon

c. Mickey Vernon

d. Chris Woodward

20. The Rangers team has played in more games than any other club that is in the American League West Division all time.

a.True

b.False

Quiz Answers

1. B - Washington Senators

2. C - 1972

3. A - True

4. A - American League West

5. C - Arlington Stadium

6. D - George W. Bush

7. C - Horse

8. D A and C (Bobby Valentine and Ron Washington each managed the Rangers for seven years.)

Chapter 7: Jerseys & Numbers

Quiz Time!

1. In 1983 in 1983, the Rangers included a logo on the jersey's front that resembled Texas. The state was represented by Texas and a big baseball as well as the letters "T.R." on top.

a.True

b.False

2. Which number was NOT removed at the Texas Rangers (as of the conclusion of the season in 2019)?

a.7

b.10

c.22

d.29

3. It was Washington Senators' colors were gold and purple.

a.True

b.False

4. What number is shortstop's uniform? Elvis Andrus wear for the Rangers?

a.4

b.3

c.2

d.1

5. What was the uniform number Nolan Ryan wear with the Rangers?

a.30

b.32

c.34

d.37

6. Who was the last player who has had his name retired from the Rangers (as of the season of 2019)?

a.Ivan Rodriguez

b. Adrian Beltre

c. Michael Young

d. Nolan Ryan

7. There is no Rangers players have ever donned the number 0 in their uniform.

a. True

b. False

8. What is the sole Rangers player ever to wear the number 84?

a. Prince Fielder

b. Rougned Odor

c. Armando Galarraga

d. Craig Gentry

9. Which ex- Rangers legend saw his number retired by the club?

a. Nolan Ryan

b. Adrian Beltre

c. Michael Young

d. Ivan Rodriguez

10. The numbers of players first appeared on the back of Rangers jerseys in the year 1984.

a. True

b. False

11. What do you think are the official colors of the Texas Rangers' official team color scheme?

a. Blue and red

b. Blue Red, black

c. Blue red and metallic gold

d. Blue Red, d.Blue, and white

12. Johnny Oates was the Rangers manager for seven years. His number was made extinct when the Rangers team was formed in shortly after his death on Christmas Eve, 2004.

a. 23

b.24

c.25

d.26

13. The Rangers have introduced alternate uniforms in powder blue with the script "Rangers" across the front the last time it was worn in 1993. The Rangers were last seen wearing uniforms in powder blue from the year 1985 to 1982.

a.True

b.False

14. Which jersey was R.A. Dickey wear as an Ranger?

a.40

b.43

c.45

d.47

15. Which jersey number was the jersey number Mark Teixeira wear as a Ranger?

a.23

b.22

c.21

d.19

16. What number of jerseys was the jersey number Juan Gonzalez wear as a Ranger?

a.16

b.19

c.14

d.12

17. Joey Gallo currently (as of the season of 2019) has the id ___ in the Rangers.

a.10

b.11

c.12

d.13

18. Which jersey Did Alex Rodriguez wear as a Ranger?

a.3

b.13

c.30

d.33

19. What number of jersey did the pitcher Yu Darvish wear as a Ranger?

a.10

b.11

c.12

d.13

20. What was the number that the second baseman Ian Kinsler wear during his time as a member of the Rangers?

a.50

b.25

c.15

d.5

Quiz Answers

1. A - True

2. C - 22

3. B - False

4. D - 1

5. C - 34

6. C - Michael Young

7. B B False, Al Oliver, Oddibe McDowell, and Junior Ortiz are among the players.

8. A - Prince Fielder

9. D - Ivan Rodriguez

10. A - True

11. D - Red, blue and white

12. D - 26

13. A - True

14. C - 45

15. A - 23

16. B - 19

17. D - 13

18. A - 3

19. B - 11

20. D - 5

Did You Know?

1. The Texas Rangers' mascot has several uniforms, which match with whatever they are wearing to the game.

2. The Rangers have resigned Ivan "Pudge" Rodriguez's number 7 Michael Young's number 10. Johnny Oates' number 26. Adrian Beltre's number 29, the number of Nolan Ryan's 44, and naturally the number 42 of Jackie Robinson.

Chapter 8: Famous Quotes

Quiz Time!

1. A former Rangers director Ron Washington was portrayed in the film "Ballpark" and the character of his said the famous phrase, "It's incredibly hard." Where is this quote taken from?

a. Trouble in the Curve

b. Million Dollar Arm

c. Moneyball

d. Fever Pitch

2. Which Former Rangers player once said "I don't really think about the number of people watching me. I'm content playing the game for me."?

a. Rafael Palmeiro

b. Vladimir Guerrero

c. Ivan Rodriguez

d. Nelson Cruz

3. Which previous Rangers manager was reported to have said "What is it in the sport world and world in general that would like to know the possibility of something happening before it actually happens? It's okay to know about it as it occurs."?

a. Ron Washington

b. Bobby Valentine

c. Johnny Oates

d. Buck Showalter

4. What former Ranger had once advised, "Discover your uniqueness; then discipline yourself to develop it."?

a. Nolan Ryan

b. Jim Sundberg

c. R.A. Dickey

d. Ivan Rodriguez

5. Which ex- Rangers player was reported to have stated, "I don't play it just to earn cash. It's simply because I enjoy the game."?

a.Josh Hamilton

b.Jose Canseco

c.Harold Baines

d.Ivan Rodriguez

6. What ex- Ranger has said that, "Enjoying success requires the capability to change. If you are open to changes will you be able to have the chance to reap maximum value from your talents."?

a.Jeff Burroughs

b.Kenny Rogers

c.Nolan Ryan

d.Bert Campaneris

7. The Former Ranger has been reported to have said "You must look at yourself at yourself in the mirror and consider how you

can aid the club. What matters is what happened today if you're losing 20 in one game. It's the next one that you'll win and I'm sure you'll be successful."?

a. Michael Young

b. Adrian Beltre

c. Nelson Cruz

d. Gerald Laird

8. The former Rangers player Charlie Hough once said, "A life is not important except in the impact it has on other lives."

a. True

b. False

9. What former Ranger was quoted to have said, "I believe a champion wins in his mind first, then plays the game, not the other way around."?

a. Ivan Rodriguez

b. Nolan Ryan

c. Alex Rodriguez

d. Ian Kinsler

10. What Former Ranger has said "I always believed that there would be a something else to do after baseball and therefore I planned that later during my lifetime I'd pursue other pursuits after baseball which I could to take on. What I did not realize was how much impact baseball played over me as well as my loved ones."?

a. Nolan Ryan

b. Michael Young

c. Johnny Oates

d. Ivan Rodriguez

11. Which ex- Ranger had said to Alex Rodriguez: "They got the top player around for the shortstop position... I'd like to be able to play alongside him. I hoped throughout the winter, hoping they would not trade my name for a player."?

a. Rafael Palmeiro

b. Michael Young

c. Mark Teixeira

d. Mike Lamb

12. The Former Ranger was quoted declaring, "I'm half Italian and my name is Portuguese. Michael Young is half Mexican. There are many players who hail from in the United States that have heritage from other places and it's a wonderful idea to hold the World Cup to celebrate the entire globe. The World Cup shows that baseball is important, and the greatness of the sport."?

a. Mark Teixeira

b. Rafael Palmeiro

c. Vladimir Guerrero

d. Bartolo Colon

13. Which player was the ex- Toronto Blue Jay Jose Bautista was referring to when he stated, "He got me pretty excellent, and I'm going to

offer him that. It takes a amount of strength to take me down" in the aftermath of their match?

a. Elvis Andrus

b. Robinson Chirinos

c. Rougned Odor

d. Jurickson Profar

14. Which ex- Rangers pitcher was reported to have said "You feel like a rock star in some ways," in reference to having been one of the Opening Day starter?

a. Mike Minor

b. Cole Hamels

c. Yu Darvish

d. Colby Lewis

15. What Former Rangers manager was said to have said "I've observed that in my life, how much you work at it and work at it, the more you improve. If you are determined to

get something and put in the effort to achieve the item, odds of success will be higher."?

a. Ted Williams

b. Don Zimmer

c. Johnny Oates

d. Jeff Banister

16. Rangers Legend Ivan "Pudge" Rodriguez once declared, "Never allow the fear of striking out keep you from playing the game."

a. True

b. False

17. Sammy Sosa is quoted as declaring, "If you have a bad day in baseball and start thinking about it, you will have ____ more."

a. No

b. Even

c. 10

d. 100

18. What ex- Rangers player said that "The biggest thing I've learned over the last few years is not looking at the big picture but focusing on that one-day-at-a-time mentality."?

a. Rafael Palmeiro

b. Mark Teixeira

c. Joey Gallo

d. Josh Hamilton

19. What previous Giants manager once said "Be anything you want to be, but don't be dull."?

a. Jim Davenport

b. Alvin Dark

c. John McGraw

d. Frank Robinson

20. Gaylord Perry once stated "The trouble with baseball is that it is not played the year round."

a. True

b. False

Quiz Answers

1. C - Moneyball

2. B - Vladimir Guerrero

3. D - Buck Showalter

4. B - Jim Sundberg

5. D - Ivan Rodriguez

6. C - Nolan Ryan

7. B - Adrian Beltre

8. B - False Jackie Robinson said this.

9. C - Alex Rodriguez

10. A - Nolan Ryan

11. B - Michael Young

12. A - Mark Teixeira

13. C - Rougned Odor

14. B - Cole Hamels

15. A - Ted Williams

16. B - False Babe Ruth said this.

17. C - 10

18. D - Josh Hamilton

19. D - Frank Robinson

20. A - True

Did You Know?

1. "Every baseball player likes fastballs similar to how everyone likes Ice cream. However, you're not a fan when somebody is putting it in your gallon. This is what you feel when you see Nolan Ryan throwing balls over you." -- Reggie Jackson

Chapter 9: Catchy Nicknames

Quiz Time!

1. What was the nickname Joey Gallo have on the back of his jersey to celebrate Players' Weekend?

a. Rooster

b. Pico de Gallo

c. Joey G

d. J Money

2. Ivan Rodriguez did not go with the nickname "Pudge" until he became a Ranger.

a. True

b. False

3. What is the nickname that the former Ranger Juan Gonzalez been going with since he was just 9 years old?

a. Juany G

b. Juan Gone

c.Igor

d.Gone Juan

4. What's the name of the former Rangers player Nolan Ryan?

a.The Ryan Express

b.The The Life of Ryan

c.Rollin' Nolan

d.Flyin' Ryan

5. What is the name that has not been used to describe that the Rangers as a group have been known by?

a.The Power Rangers

b.The Rags

c.The Lone Stars

d.The Blue and Red

6. What was the nickname Adrian Beltre's father give to him when he was a child?

a. Belty

b. Estrella

c. Kojak

d. Gran Chico

7. The nickname of Kenny Rogers used to be "The Gambler," after the song of the artist with his same name.

a. True

b. False

8. What is the nickname that the former Ranger Nelson Cruz go by?

a. Aplastar

b. Fuerte

c. Dominican Dandy

d. Boomstick

9. In 2017's MLB Players' Weekend, which nickname did the former Rangers player Jason Grilli wear on the reverse of his shirt?

a. Put it on the Grill

b. Grill cheese

c. All down in my Grill

d. Grill Chicken

10. What nickname did the MLB Hall of Fame as well as ex- Ranger Vladimir Guerrero NOT go with during his time in the MLB?

a. Vlad the Impaler

b. Big Daddy Vladdy

c. Make "'Em Sad, Vlad

d. Big Bad Vlad

11. "Goose" is his nickname. What's the true name of the former Rangers player Goose Gossage?

a. Maxwell William

b. Richard Michael

c. Kevin Arthur

d. Bartholomew Robert

12. Former Rangers player Cliff Lee's initial name was Clifton.

a. True

b. False

13. Jarrod Saltalamacchia's final name, with 14 letters is the longest name ever recorded in MLB history. It translates to "jump over" in Italian. What was the nickname of Saltalamacchia?

a. Salt

b. Mach

c. J Salt

d. Salty

14. What's the name of the former Rangers player Derek Holland?

a. Holly

b. Dutch Oven

c. Dutch Derek

d. Daunting Derek

15. A former ranger Will Clark was known with the moniker "Will the Thrill."

a. True

b. False

16. What's the name of the name of former Rangers player C.J. Wilson's real name?

a. Cody James Wilson

b. Christopher James Wilson

c. Christopher John Wilson

d. Cody John Wilson

17. A former Rangers player Michael Young went by the name "Young Blood."

a. True

b. False

18. A former Rangers manager Showalter has the name "Buck." What is the real name of his manager?

a. Bruce Nathaniel Showalter III

b. Bruce William Showalter III

c. William Edward Showalter III

d. William Nathaniel Showalter III

19. In 2017's MLB Players' Weekend, which nickname did the former Rangers player A.J. Griffin wear on his back jersey?

a. Arthur Joseph

b. Griff

c. Sweet Lettuce

d. HAIR

20. What's the name of the former Rangers 1st baseman Mark Teixeira?

a. Tex

b. Marky T

c. Tex Mex

d. M.T.

Quiz Answers 1. B - Pico de Gallo

2. A - True

3. C Igor Igor (He was fascinated by a wrestler, Igor the Magnificent, while the time he was just a little kid.)

4. A - The Ryan Express

5. D - The Blue and Red

6. C C Kojak (That is the title of a hairless detective in the TV show in the time Even when a child, Adrian didn't have much hair.)

Chapter 10: The Ryan Express

Quiz Time!

1. What's the complete Nolan Ryan name?

a.Nolan Lyle Ryan Jr.

b.Lyle Nolan Ryan Jr.

c.Lynn Nolan Ryan Jr.

d.Nolan Lynn Ryan Jr.

2. In the course of his MLB time, Nolan Ryan played for the Texas Rangers, Houston Astros, New York Mets, as well as the California Angels.

a.True

b.False

3. In which country was Nolan Ryan born?

a.Houston, Texas

b.Refugio, Texas

c.Frisco, Texas

d. Dallas, Texas

4. The year of Nolan Ryan born?

a. January 13, 1947

b. January 13, 1950

c. January 31, 1950

d. January 31, 1947

5. Nolan Ryan threw seven no-hitters during the course of his MLB career.

a. True

b. False

6. What number of MLB records do Nolan Ryan currently hold?

a. 61

b. 51

c. 41

d. 31

7. What was the place where Nolan Ryan go to high school?

a.Alvin High School

b.Clear The Creek High School

c.Westwood High School

d.Carroll High School

8. In the year that Nolan Ryan was called up to the New York Mets in 1966 at the age of 22, he was the 2nd-youngest athlete in MLB.

a.True

b.False

9. Nolan Ryan was previously _____ from The Texas Rangers organization.

a.General manager

b.CEO

c.Executive advisor

d.Head Scout

10. What's the title of Nolan Ryan's autobiography from 1992?

a. Nolan Ryan's Pitcher's Book

b. Throwing the heat

c. Miracle Man

d. The Road to Cooperstown

11. Nolan Ryan played in the MLB during how many president administrations?

a. 3

b. 5

c. 7

d. 9

12. Nolan Ryan is one of the 3 players from MLB time to see had his team's uniform number removed by three teams.

Chapter 11: Statistically Speaking

Quiz Time!

1. Juan Gonzalez holds the Texas Rangers franchise record for highest number of home runs. How many of them did Juan Gonzalez strike?

a.321

b.372

c.246

d.217

2. Pitcher Charlie Hough has the most wins in Texas Rangers franchise history, having 139 wins.

a.True

b.False

3. What is the most recent time that the Rangers been to the playoffs?

a.8 times

b. 10 times

c. 12 times

d. 7 times

4. Who is the Rangers single-season record of Doubles in the year 2006 with 52?

a. Elvis Andrus

b. Michael Young

c. Mark Teixeira

d. Nelson Cruz

5. Which pitcher is most prolific in strikes in Rangers team history with 1,452?

a. Kenny Rogers

b. Yu Darvish

c. Nolan Ryan

d. Charlie Hough

6. Juan Gonzalez has the most RBI ever recorded in Rangers franchise history. his _____.

a.984

b.1,230

c.1,180

d.842

7. Bobby Valentine is the Rangers greatest manager to win the championships.

a.True

b.False

8. What player has the record for most saved games during the history of a franchise, totalling 150?

a.Neftali Feliz

b.John Wetteland

c.C.J. Wilson

d.Joe Nathan

9. Who is the Rangers franchise record in stolen bases, which is 302?

a. Elvis Andrus

b. Ian Kinsler

c. Delino DeShields

d. Bump Wills

10. Who is the single season Rangers records for the most hits at 221?

a. Mickey Rivers

b. Rafael Palmeiro

c. Alex Rodriguez

d. Michael Young

11. Who is the holder of the single-season Rangers record in home runs, holding the most?

a. Frank Howard

b. Juan Gonzalez

c. Alex Rodriguez

d. Rafael Palmeiro

12. Adrian Beltre hit the most sacrifice fly in Rangers franchise the history of Rangers franchise.

a. True

b. False

13. Who was the pitcher who threw one of the highest number of wild pitches throughout Rangers club history, totalling 99?

a. Bobby Witt

b. Nolan Ryan

c. Charlie Hough

d. Kevin Brown

14. Who is the Rangers single-season record in the most triples in a single season, 14?

a. Ruben Sierra

b. Marty Keough

c. Chuck Hinton

d. Rougned Odor

15. Who has had the highest number of walks in Rangers franchise history with 805?

a. Shin-Soo Choo

b. Rusty Greer

c. Mike Hargrove

d. Rafael Palmeiro

16. Which Rangers player has the single-season record for the most strikeouts at more than 207?

a. Mike Napoli

b. Joey Gallo

c. Josh Hamilton

d. Ian Desmond

17. Michael Young has the most hits, doubles and triples recorded in Rangers the history of the franchise.

a. True

b. False

18. Who has had the most plate appearances throughout Rangers team history, totalling 8,047?

a. Ivan Rodriguez

b. Elvis Andrus

c. Michael Young

d. Adrian Beltre

19. Who is the holder of the Rangers franchise record for the most saves during a single season?

a. Joe Nathan

b. Neftali Feliz

c. John Wetteland

d. Francisco Cordero

20. Kenny Rogers allowed the most hits during Rangers franchise history with 1,997.

a. True

b. False

Quiz Answers

1. B - 372

2. A - True

3. 8x

4. B - Michael Young

5. D - Charlie Hough

6. C - 1,180

7. B - False Ron Washington holds that record.

8. B - John Wetteland

9. A - Elvis Andrus

10. D - Michael Young

11. C - Alex Rodriguez

12. B - False Michael Young holds that record.

13. C - Charlie Hough

14. A - Ruben Sierra

15. D - Rafael Palmeiro

16. B - Joey Gallo

17. A - True

18. C - Michael Young

19. D - Francisco Cordero

20. A - True

Did You Know?

1. Charlie Hough threw the most innings of Rangers team history, throwing 2,308 innings. The second place spot in third place is Kenny Rogers with 1,909 innings.

2. Al Oliver has the best lifetime batting percentage in Rangers franchise history, at .319. Will Clark is second with an average of .308.

3. Ian Kinsler holds the Rangers franchise record for steal bases, at 80.37 percent performance. Elvis Andrus holds the franchise

record for the most stolen bases ever at 302 and the number of times he was stolen bases, which is the record of 104.

4. Juan Gonzalez has the most Extra-base hits throughout Rangers the history of the franchise, having 713. Next on the list comes Rafael Palmeiro with 667.

5. Alex Rodriguez holds the Rangers record for the most at-bats in a home run at 11.9. In his time in Texas Alex Rodriguez hit a home run in every 11-12 at-bats.

6. Craig Gentry, Jurickson Profar Jurickson Profar, Craig Gentry and Michael Young are all tied with Michael Young for Michael Young, Jurickson Profar, and Craig Gentry are tied for Rangers record in a single season for stolen base percentage of 100! Through the entire year, they weren't removed from the field after they stole bases. Incredible!

Chapter 12: The Trade Market

Quiz Time!

1. The deadline for trades was 2007 the Rangers purchased Jarrod Saltalamacchia Elvis Andrus, Matt Harrison, Neftali Feliz, and Beau Jones from the Atlanta Braves as part of a trade for _____ along with Ron Mahay.

a. Nelson Cruz

b. Sammy Sosa

c. Mark Teixeira

d. Marlon Byrd

2. On the 19th of July, 2000 On the 19th of July, 2000, the Rangers exchanged Esteban Loaiza over to Toronto Blue Jays. Toronto Blue Jays in exchange in exchange for _____ as well as Darwin Cubillan.

a. Rafael Palmeiro

b. Kenny Rogers

c. Ivan Rodriguez

d. Michael Young

3. In December 2007 Josh Hamilton was traded to the Rangers by the Cincinnati Reds.

a. True

b. False

4. On the 16th of February in 2004, the Rangers bought Alfonso Soriano and Joaquin Arias from the New York Yankees in exchange in exchange for _____.

a. Juan Gonzalez

b. Alex Rodriguez

c. Ryan Christenson

d. Rafael Palmeiro

5. In 2015 at the deadline for trades in 2015, the Rangers traded six players for Cole Hamels and Jake Diekman.

a. True

b. False

6. Which year was the Rangers make the trade Juan Gonzalez to the Detroit Tigers?

a.1997

b.1998

c.1999

d.2000

7. In 1989 In 1989, the Rangers swapped _____, Wilson Alvarez, and Scott Fletcher to the Chicago White Sox in exchange for Harold Baines and Fred Manrique.

a.Cecil Espy

b.Ruben Sierra

c.Rick Leach

d.Sammy Sosa

8. Which team sold Cliff Lee to the Rangers in the year 2010?

a.Cleveland Indians

b. Philadelphia Phillies

c. Seattle Mariners

d. Tampa Bay Rays

9. The 31st of August, 1992 the Rangers exchanged Ruben Sierra Bobby Witt, and Jeff Russell to the Oakland A's in exchange for _____.

a. Jose Canseco

b. Rickey Henderson

c. Mark McGwire

d. Dave Stewart

10. To get Jeff Kent in 1996, the Giants traded the third baseman Matt Williams to the Cleveland Indians.

a. True

b. False

11. On the 20th of November in 2013 The Rangers made a trade of Ian Kinsler to the Detroit Tigers in exchange for_____.

a. Miguel Cabrera

b. Prince Fielder

c. Austin Jackson

d. Brandon Inge

12. The Rangers have (as as of) completed just three trades with Arizona Diamondbacks ever.

a. True

b. False

13. What are the most trades that the Rangers completed together with their Houston Astros all time (as at the close of the season in 2019)?

a. 3

b. 10

c. 12

d. 15

14. The Rangers never made an exchange against Washington Nationals. Washington Nationals.

a. True

b. False

15. After five seasons with the Rangers, Josh Hamilton signed as a free-agent with the Los Angeles Angels of Anaheim. In the year 2015, he was traded back to Rangers in exchange for the Angels.

a. True

b. False

16. The deadline for trades was 2017 the Rangers made a trade with the Los Angeles Dodgers in exchange for A.J. Alexy, Brendon Davis, and Willie Calhoun.

a. Andrew Cashner

b. Cole Hamels

c. A.J. Griffin

d. Yu Darvish

17. On the 7th of August, 2015, the_____ sent Mike Napoli and cash to the Rangers in exchange for a player who will be named in the future and cash.

a. Boston Red Sox

b. Los Angeles Angels from Anaheim

c. Cleveland Indians

d. New York Yankees

18. The 15th of December in 2019 The Cleveland Indians traded _____ and cash with the Rangers in exchange for Delino DeShields as well as Emmanuel Clase.

a. Lance Lynn

b. Mike Minor

c. Corey Kluber

d. Drew Smyly

19. The Rangers have participated in ___ trades in the past with Colorado Rockies in franchise history (as in June, 2020).

a. 1

b. 5

c. 8

d. 19

20. In June of 2003 the Rangers made a trade of Ruben Sierra for the New York Yankees in exchange in exchange for Marcus Thames.

a. True

b. False

Quiz Answers

1. C - Mark Teixeira

2. D - Michael Young

3. A - True

4. B - Alex Rodriguez

5. A - True

6. C - 1999

7. D - Sammy Sosa

8. C - Seattle Mariners

9. A - Jose Canseco

10. A - True

11. B - Prince Fielder

12. A - True

13. B - 10

14. B - False

15. A - True

16. D - Yu Darvish

17. A - Boston Red Sox

18. C - Corey Kluber

19. B - 5

20. A - True

Did You Know?

1. The Texas Rangers had the 20th most payroll of any team in Major League Baseball in 2019 in the amount of $106.96 million. They were followed by the Chicago Cubs held the spot with the most payroll, at more than $211 million.

2. On the 9th of December on 2012 on December 9, 2012, the Rangers made a trade of Michael Young and cash to the Philadelphia Phillies in exchange for Lisalverto Bonilla and Josh Lindblom.

3. Nolan Ryan signed as a free agent by the Texas Rangers on December 7 in 1988. Ryan's career ended with the Rangers in 1993.

4. The Rangers have traded 14 times in the last 14 years with San Francisco Giants all time (as in June 2020).

Chapter 13: Draft Day

Quiz Time!

1. In the overall draft, which was held in the first draft of the 2001 MLB Draft, the Texas Rangers chose the infielder Mark Teixeira.

a.1st

b.2nd

c.5th

d.10th

2. In the 18th round in the 1st selection round of 1996's MLB Draft, the Texas Rangers chose _____.

a.Carlos Pena

b.R.A. Dickey

c.Kevin Brown

d.Bobby Witt

3. As the 11th overall selection in the first stage of 2008's MLB Draft, the Texas Rangers

chose the first baseman Justin Smoak from _____.

a.Clemson University

b.University of South Carolina

c.College of Charleston

d.University of North Carolina Chapel Hill

4. The overall selection was ___ during the 1st selection stage of 1969's MLB Draft, the Texas Rangers picked the outfielder Jeff Burroughs.

a.1st

b.3rd

c.4th

d.9th

5. The 4th overall selection during the first round in the MLB Draft in 2015 MLB Draft, the Texas Rangers picked their pitcher Dillon Tate from _____.

a.UC Davis

b. UCLA

c. UC San Diego

d. UC Santa Barbara

6. Pitcher Ron Darling was drafted by the Texas Rangers in the _____ round of the 1981 MLB Draft out of Yale University.

a. 3rd

b. 6th

c. 9th

d. 11th

7. The Texas Rangers drafted Joey Gallo in the 1st Round in the 2012 MLB Draft, 39th overall. Instead of registering at LSU the team signed him to the Rangers to receive the $2.25 million sign-on bonus.

a. True

b. False

8. Pitcher Kenny Rogers was drafted in the 39th Round of the ____ MLB Draft by the Texas Rangers.

a. 1980

b. 1981

c. 1982

d. 1983

9. First overall selection in the 1st round 1999 MLB draft, the team _____ picked player in the field Josh Hamilton.

a. Texas Rangers

b. Los Angeles Angels from Anaheim

c. Tampa Bay Devil Rays

d. Cincinnati Reds

10. Harold Baines was drafted 1st overall in the first round of 1977's MLB Draft by the Chicago White Sox.

a. True

b.False

11. The 8th round in the 1996 MLB Draft, the _____ chosen pitcher was Charlie Hough.

a.Florida Marlins

b.Los Angeles Dodgers

c.Chicago White Sox

d.Texas Rangers

12. Alex Rodriguez was drafted 1st overall in the 1st Round of 1993's MLB Draft by the Seattle Mariners.

a.True

b.False

13. The Texas Rangers selected pitcher _____ during the 25th round during the MLB Draft.

a.Jason Grilli

b.C.J. Wilson

c. Brandon McCarthy

d. Derek Holland

14. The Texas Rangers selected pitcher _____ in the 5th selection round during the 2001 MLB Draft.

a. R.A. Dickey

b. C.J. Wilson

c. Kenny Rogers

d. Scott Feldman

15. Present Texas Rangers manager Chris Woodward was picked during the 54th round of 1994's MLB Draft by the _____.

a. New York Mets

b. Boston Red Sox

c. Toronto Blue Jays

d. Atlanta Braves

16. The former Texas Rangers pitcher Cole Hamels was selected in the 1st Round of 2002's MLB Draft by the _____.

a. Chicago Cubs

b. Philadelphia Phillies

c. Los Angeles Dodgers

d. New York Yankees

17. In the 17th round of 2007 MLB Draft, the Texas Rangers picked _____.

a. Geovany Soto

b. Ian Kinsler

c. Craig Gentry

d. Mitch Moreland

18. Which college was the First Baseman Carlos Pena drafted out of?

a. Boston College

b. Harvard University

c.Northeastern University

d.University of Massachusetts, Boston

19. The 1st selection stage of 2020's MLB Draft, the Texas Rangers chose first baseman _____ as 14th overall from Mississippi State.

a.Justin Foscue

b.Evan Carter

c.Tekoah Roby

d.Dylan MacLean

20. Rafael Palmeiro was drafted by the New York Mets in the 8th Round of the 1982 MLB Draft and then again in the 22nd Round of the 1985 MLB Draft by the Chicago Cubs.

a.True

b.False

Chapter 14: Odds & Ends

Quiz Time!

1. Adrian Beltre hates when people are able to touch his _____.

a. Feet

b. Shoulder

c. Ear

d. Head

2. Prince Fielder was named after the famous musician Prince due to his mother being an avid fan of the artist.

a. True

b. False

3. In May of 1993 Jose Canseco let a fly ball bounce off of his _____ and over his outfield wall. This resulted in a homerun for Cleveland Indians infielder Carlos Martinez.

a. Arm

b.Leg

c.Head

d.Foot

4. Which ex- Ranger is prone to a nap prior to nearly every game he participates during a pregame ritual?

a.Yu Darvish

b.Mitch Moreland

c.Ian Kinsler

d.Nelson Cruz

5. At the age of 8 old, the former Ranger Prince Fielder starred in the commercial for _____. He slapped his father Cecil an ex-MLB player in his own right.

a.Chevrolet

b.McDonald's

c.Coca-Cola

d.Disneyland

6. Which previous Ranger has coached for the American League in the 2010 Taco Bell All-Star Legends & Celebrity Softball Game?

a. Goose Gossage

b. Nolan Ryan

c. Ivan Rodriguez

d. Kenny Rogers

7. A former Rangers player Jose Canseco has a twin brother, who played with the MLB.

a. True

b. False

8. A former Ranger Adrian Gonzalez's son-in-law (his spouse's brother) is also a player in the MLB. What is his brother-in law's name?

a. Bryce Harper

b. Kris Bryant

c. Manny Machado

d. Clayton Kershaw

9. Which of the former Ranger made an appearance in the Guitar Hero World Tour commercial singing guitar along with Kobe Bryant on vocals, Michael Phelps on bass, and Tony Hawk on drums?

a. Nolan Ryan

b. Alex Rodriguez

c. Adrian Beltre

d. Ivan Rodriguez

10. A former Rangers pitching coach Yu Darvish can guess someone's _____ by engaging in conversations with them, as well as getting to know their character.

a. Favorite color

b. Astrological sign

c. Age

d. Blood kind

11. The former Rangers player Derek Holland was once kicked out of a concert located in New Jersey.

a. One Direction

b. Bruce Springsteen

c. Counting Crows

d. Ariana Grande

12. The former Ranger Fergie Jenkins was also a basketball player with the Harlem Globetrotters.

a. True

b. False

13. What is it that Josh Hamilton have tattooed on his left arm?

a. A Portrait of Alexander Hamilton

b. "Hambone"

c. A porc

d. "Hammy"

14. What ex- Ranger has become an analyst on MLB Network?

a.Mark DeRosa

b.Tim Lincecum

c.Aubrey Huff

d.Cody Ross

15. What country artist Did Rangers fielder Elvis Andrus listen to when the teen years came to aid him in learning English?

a.Carrie Underwood

b.Shania Twain

c.Rascal Flatts

d.Tim McGraw

16. The same owner that relocated basketball's Lakers to Minneapolis into Los Angeles was the owner who relocated his team the Rangers out of Washington in Washington to Arlington.

a.True

b. False

17. The former Rangers pitching coach C.J. Wilson hosts a benefit annual event that features the most popular game on video?

a. Mario Party

b. Fortnite

c. Call of Duty

d. Guitar Hero

18. What city do the Rangers Double-A squad play?

a. Sacramento, California

b. Indianapolis, Indiana

c. Sioux Falls, South Dakota

d. Frisco, Texas

19. Who was the first and the only Rangers pitcher to pitch an exact game?

a. Kenny Rogers

b. Nolan Ryan

c. Cole Hamels

d. Yu Darvish

20. A former Rangers catcher Taylor Teagarden won a bronze medal during the 2008 Summer Olympics in Beijing as a player of the USA baseball team.

a. True

b. False

Quiz Answers

1. D - Head

2. A - True

3. C - Head

4. D - Nelson Cruz

5. B - McDonald's

6. A - Goose Gossage

Chapter 15: Outfielders

Quiz Time!

1. Which team did ex- Rangers infielder Nelson Cruz NOT played for in his entire career (as as of the season in 2019)?

a.Milwaukee Brewers

b.Detroit Tigers

c.Seattle Mariners

d.Baltimore Orioles

2. In 1974, ex- Rangers fielder Jeff Burroughs led the American League in RBI and was awarded the American League MVP Award.

a.True

b.False

3. What team did the former Rangers player Juan Gonzalez NOT play for in his professional career?

a.Cleveland Indians

b. Kansas City Royals

c. Detroit Tigers

d. Florida Marlins

4. The current Ranger Joey Gallo became the fastest player in American League history to hit 100 home runs.

a. True

b. False

5. A former Rangers fielder Gabe Kapler is now manager of what MLB team?

a. New York Mets

b. Washington Nationals

c. San Francisco Giants

d. Houston Astros

6. What was the total number of games that outfielder Delino deShields take part in his first season in 2015? (first) season for the Rangers?

a.80

b.121

c.162

d.137

7. Shin-Soo Choo is a player who has spent all of his professional career (as as of the season in 2019) for Shin-Soo Choo and the Texas Rangers.

a.True

b.False

8. What was the length of time Jose Canseco play for the Rangers?

a.1

b.2

c.3

d.4

9. What was the number of home runs Hunter Pence hit during his playing time during his

time with the Texas Rangers during the 2019 season?

a. 8

b. 18

c. 28

d. 1

10. How many seasons did the outfielder Josh Hamilton play for the Texas Rangers?

a. 6

b. 7

c. 8

d. 9

11. What team did the former Rangers infielder Craig Gentry NOT play for in his 10 year MLB career?

a. Oakland A's

b. Los Angeles Angels from Anaheim

c. Baltimore Orioles

d. San Diego Padres

12. David Murphy never had more than 10 home runs in his time playing for his team, the Texas Rangers.

a. True

b. False

13. Mitch Moreland has so far (as of the year 2019) played for a different MLB team, apart from the Rangers. Which team are they on?

a. Los Angeles Dodgers

b. Minnesota Twins

c. Boston Red Sox

d. Atlanta Braves

14. Son of former Ranger Vladimir Guerrero, Vladimir Guerrero Jr. is now (as as of the season in 2019) is a third baseman for what MLB team?

a. Los Angeles Angels from Anaheim

b. Toronto Blue Jays

c. Baltimore Orioles

d. Texas Rangers

15. What was Rangers Outfielder Alfonso Sóriano's with the Rangers in 2004?

a. .277

b. .260

c. .280

d. .236

16. Sammy Sosa hit only one home run in his time with the Rangers as well as 21 homers during his time as a member of the Rangers.

a. True

b. False

17. How many runs did the outfielder Marlon Byrd collect during his time with the Rangers in 2009?

a. 135

b.145

c.155

d.165

18. What team did the former Rangers player Jeff Burroughs NOT play for in his entire 16-year MLB professional career?

a.Oakland A's

b.Atlanta Braves

c.Seattle Mariners

d.Chicago Cubs

19. What number of MLB All-Star Games did former Rangers outfielder Alex Rios play in during his playing career?

a.0

b.2

c.3

d.4

20. A former Rangers player in the outfield Marlon Byrd was with 10 distinct MLB teams over the course of his entire 15-season MLB career.

a. True

b. False

Quiz Answers

1. B - Detroit Tigers

2. A - True

3. D - Florida Marlins

4. A - True

5. C - San Francisco Giants

6. B - 121

7. B - False also played for his team the Seattle Mariners, Cleveland Indians as well as the Cincinnati Reds.

8. C - 3

9. B - 18

10. A - 6

11. D - San Diego Padres

12. B - False

13. C - Boston Red Sox

14. B - Toronto Blue Jays

15. C - .280

16. A - True

17. C - 155

18. D - Chicago Cubs

19. B - 2

Chapter 16: Infielders

Quiz Time!

1. What was the number of games the former Rangers third-baseman Adrian Beltre play in during his time on the team?

a.999

b.1,001

c.1,232

d.1,098

2. The end of the 2019 season the former Rangers 2nd baseman Ian Kinsler has appeared in four All-Star Games. The majority of them included the Rangers.

a.True

b.False

3. What number of games did the former Rangers Infielder Michael Young play in during his 13 years in the club?

a.1,101

b.1,823

c.2,098

d.1,458

4. Alex Rodriguez played for the Texas Rangers for three seasons as well as, naturally was part of the New York Yankees for 12 years. Alex Rodriguez played for a total of three teams in the span of his 22-season career. What different MLB organization did he represent with?

a.Florida Marlins

b.San Diego Padres

c.Seattle Mariners

d.Los Angeles Dodgers

5. What MLB team did the former Rangers First Baseman Mark Teixeira NOT play for throughout his career of 14 seasons?

a.New York Yankees

b.Atlanta Braves

c. Toronto Blue Jays

d. Los Angeles Angels from Anaheim

6. What was the length of time Prince Fielder have during his time in the MLB?

a. 10

b. 12

c. 14

d. 18

7. Michael Young played his entire MLB career as a player for his team, the Texas Rangers.

a. True

b. False

8. What was the number of home runs the former Ranger Lance Berkman score during his single season (73 games) while playing for the team?

a. 6

b. 12

c.20

d.24

9. What was the number of home runs Rangers shortstop Elvis Andrus hit during the 2017 season?

a.22

b.25

c.20

d.29

10. In the course of his career over 21 seasons in the Rangers, the former Rangers 3rd baseman Adrian Beltre appeared in ___ MLB All-Star Games, and the team received the team with four Silver Slugger Awards and five Gold Glove Awards.

a.2

b.3

c.4

d.7

11. What number of hit did the former Rangers 1st baseman Mitch Moreland accumulate during his seven years in Texas?

a.633

b.643

c.653

d.663

12. Rougned Odor appeared in every single game played by the Rangers in 2017.

a.True

b.False

13. What was the place that the former Rangers First Baseman Rafael Palmeiro born?

a.Puerto Rico

b.Cuba

c.Spain

d.Dominican Republic

14. What was the number of games that the first baseman play? Will Clark play for the Rangers in the 1995 season?

a. 101

b. 112

c. 132

d. 123

15. What was the length of time Rafael Palmeiro play for the Texas Rangers?

a. 8

b. 10

c. 12

d. 13

16. The former Rangers 3rd baseman Buddy Bell was NEVER named to the MLB All-Star Game during his professional career.

a. True

b. False

17. Which of the infielders did not play with BOTH the Rangers and the Houston Astros during his MLB time?

a.Lance Berkman

b.Ryan Theriot

c.Mark Teixeira

d.Buddy Bell

18. Which of the infielders did not play with BOTH the Rangers and the Oakland A's during his MLB time?

a.Mike Hargrove

b.Bert Campaneris

c.Kevin Kouzmanoff

d.Jurickson Profar

19. Shortstop Elvis Andrus was named to the MLB All-Star Game in 2010 and also _____.

a.2011

b.2012

c.2014

d.2018

20. A former Rangers 1st baseman Mike Hargrove was named the American League Rookie of the Year in the year 1974.

a.True

b.False

Quiz Answers

1. D - 1,098

2. A - True

3. B - 1,823

4. C - Seattle Mariners

5. C - Toronto Blue Jays

6. B - 12

7. B - False. He was also with his team the Philadelphia Phillies and Los Angeles Dodgers.

8. A - 6

9. C 20 (His highest career mark in just one season, as of the 2019 season.)

10. C - 4

11. A - 633

12. A - True

13. B - Cuba

14. D - 123

15. B - 10

16. B - False was selected to the five All-Star Games (1973, 1980 1981 1982, 1983,).

17. C - Mark Teixeira

18. A - Mike Hargrove

19. B - 2012

20. A - True

Did You Know?

1. Rangers Second baseman Rougned Odor was named the American League Player of the Week on the 26th of July 2015. September 4 2016, the 22nd of July, 2018, and, on August 5, 2018.

2. The former Rangers premier baseman Rafael Palmeiro was named the American League Player of the Week on May 28th 1989, July 12 in 1992 July 4 1, 1993; August 1 in 1993, and on August 22, 1999.

3. At the close of the season in 2019, at the time of this writing, shortstop Elvis Andrus has appeared in two MLB All-Star Games.

4. The former Rangers player infielder Michael Young only won one Gold Glove Award in his time with the Rangers.

5. A former Rangers First baseman Will Clark also played for the San Francisco Giants, Baltimore Orioles in addition to the St. Louis Cardinals during his 15-season MLB career.

Chapter 17: Pitchers & Catchers

Quiz Time!

1. What was the number of strikeouts Nolan Ryan record during his 1989 season as a player for the Rangers?

a.341

b.223

c.301

d.327

2. Ivan "Pudge" Rodriguez hit 217 home runs during the course of 13 seasons as a player with the Rangers.

a.True

b.False

3. Which pitcher hasn't been a part of BOTH the Rangers as well as the Houston Astros in his MLB career?

a.Armando Galarraga

b. Travis Blackley

c. Cole Hamels

d. Nolan Ryan

4. Which of the former Rangers manager had an catcher during his playing professional career?

a. Ron Washington

b. Don Zimmer

c. Bobby Valentine

d. Jeff Banister

5. Which pitcher hasn't played for BOTH the Rangers as well as the Seattle Mariners in their MLB professional career?

a. Goose Gossage

b. Neftali Feliz

c. R.A. Dickey

d. Cliff Lee

6. What number of stops Did Joe Nathan record for the Rangers in the 2013 season?

a.37

b.43

c.46

d.32

7. R.A. Dickey was named to just an MLB All-Star Game in his professional career.

a.True

b.False

8. Kenny Rogers was awarded ___ Gold Gloves during his 20-season MLB career.

a.3

b.4

c.5

d.6

9. What was the total number of games that the catcher A.J. Pierzynski take part in for the Rangers in 2013?

a. 101

b. 110

c. 121

d. 134

10. Was Cole Hamels's win-loss record in the season of 2016 as a member of the Rangers?

a. 15-5

b. 12-8

c. 13-7

d. 14-6

11. The 1st day of May 1991, _____ pitched one of the first Rangers no-hitter in their home.

a. Kenny Rogers

b. Nolan Ryan

c. Bobby Witt

d. Goose Gossage

12. A former Rangers director Johnny Oates played for the Rangers throughout his MLB time as an catcher.

a. True

b. False

13. What was the number of games C.J. Wilson begin with the Rangers in 2011?

a. 28

b. 31

c. 33

d. 34

14. What number of MLB All-Star Games was former Rangers Goose Gossage, a pitcher from the Rangers, referred to during his 22-season baseball career?

a. 3

b.9

c.10

d.11

15. What MLB team did the former Rangers pitching coach John Wetteland NOT play for in his time?

a.Montreal Expos

b.Los Angeles Dodgers

c.New York Yankees

d.Colorado Rockies

16. Ivan "Pudge" Rodriguez was indicted for 127 passes throughout his professional career.

a.True

b.False

17. What was the number of complete games Derek Holland throw for the Rangers in the year 2011?

a. 4

b. 2

c. 1

d. 0

18. What was the number of intentional walks the former Rangers player Yu Darvish throw during the 2013 season?

a. 0

b. 1

c. 4

d. 5

19. Did Colby Lewis throw as many wild pitches? Colby Lewis throw in his 2010 season for the Rangers?

a. 0

b. 3

c. 6

d. 9

20. In the eight seasons that Scott Feldman playing for the Rangers the team, he posted the winning percentage in just two.

a. True

b. False

Quiz Answers

1. C - 301

2. A - True

3. C - Cole Hamels

4. D - Jeff Banister

5. B - Neftali Feliz

6. B - 43

7. A - True

8. C - 5

9. D - 134

10. A - 15-5

11. B - Nolan Ryan

12. B-False was a player with The Atlanta Braves, Los Angeles Dodgers, Philadelphia Phillies, New York Yankees, and Baltimore Orioles.

13. D - 34

14. B - 9

15. D - Colorado Rockies

16. A - True

17. A - 4

18. B - 1

19. D - 9

20. A - True

Did You Know? 1. Present Rangers Catcher Jeff Mathis has been in the MLB for fifteen seasons (as as of the year the year 2019). He also has played for the Los Angeles Angels of Anaheim as well as the Miami Marlins, the

Arizona Diamondbacks and the Toronto Blue Jays.

2. Present Rangers pitching Mike Minor was named to the 2019 MLB All-Star Game as a part of the Rangers.

3. Bartolo Colon pitched for the Rangers in the season of 2018 at 45. His MLB debut was in 1997 for the Cleveland Indians. He was also a part of The Los Angeles Angels of Anaheim, New York Mets, Oakland A's, Chicago White Sox, Minnesota Twins, Atlanta Braves, Boston Red Sox, New York Yankees as well as The Montreal Expos. He's affectionately referred to as "Big Sexy."

4. For 11 years playing for the Texas Rangers, Bobby Witt's performance record for pitching was precisely .500 with a 104-104 record.

5. Hall of Fame pitcher Goose Gossage played in the Rangers in the year 1991. The team also included The Oakland A's, New York Yankees, Chicago White Sox, Pittsburgh Pirates, San Diego Padres, San Francisco Giants, Chicago

Cubs, as well as the Seattle Mariners during his 22-season career.

6. Kenny Rogers threw the only perfect pitch that has ever been played in Rangers history (as as of the season 2019).

7. Jose Canseco pitched in one game with his team the Rangers back in the year 1993. He pitched one innings, allowed two hits, and earned three runs. In the inning, he faced eight batters but took three walks. His ERA was 27.00.

8. Jamie Moyer pitched two seasons with his team, the Texas Rangers. The 25-season MLB time, Jamie Moyer was a player for his team the Colorado Rockies, Seattle Mariners, Chicago Cubs, Philadelphia Phillies, Baltimore Orioles, St. Louis Cardinals, and Boston Red Sox. Over the course of his career in the MLB, he was a part of an appearance at the MLB All-Star Game only once.

9. In the 1987 season, Rangers pitcher Charlie Hough pitched 13 complete games. He played

in 40 games, and then completed 40 games. He pitched 285.1 innings and faced a batter for 1,231 innings.

10. Charlie Hough gave up the largest number of home runs during Rangers franchise history by 238. Next to last comes Kenny Rogers with 195 home runs he gave up.

Chapter 18: World Series

Quiz Time!

1. Which World Series have the Texas Rangers been a part of?

a. 0

b. 2

c. 4

d. 5

2. Which AL pennants has been awarded to the Texas Rangers won?

a. 1

b. 2

c. 3

d. 4

3. What teams was it that the Texas Rangers face in the 2010 World Series?

a. St. Louis Cardinals

b. Los Angeles Dodgers

c. San Francisco Giants

d. Washington Nationals

4. What teams faced the Texas Rangers face in the 2011 World Series?

a. St. Louis Cardinals

b. Los Angeles Dodgers

c. San Francisco Giants

d. Washington Nationals

5. It was the Texas Rangers' only wild card slot came from the year _____.

a. 2015

b. 2014

c. 2013

d. 2012

6. What was the total number of games played in this year's World Series go?

a. 4

b. 5

c. 6

d. 7

7. Nelson Cruz was named the 2011 ALCS MVP of the 2011 ALCS.

a. True

b. False

8. Which was Texas Rangers' manager when they reached their way to the World Series in 2010 and 2011.

a. Buck Showalter

b. Ron Washington

c. Jeff Banister

d. Bobby Valentine

9. What was the total number of games played in the World Series in 2010? World Series go?

a. 4

b. 5

c. 6

d. 7

10. Who was the one who started the game 1 in the 2010 World Series for the Rangers?

a. C.J. Wilson

b. Colby Lewis

c. Cliff Lee

d. Derek Holland

11. Who was the pitcher who played the game 1 in the 2011 World Series for the Rangers?

a. C.J. Wilson

b. Scott Feldman

c. Colby Lewis

d. Derek Holland

12. Vladimir Guerrero was named the MVP for the 2010 ALCS MVP of the 2010 ALCS.

a. True

b. False

13. What number of American League West titles have the Texas Rangers won (as of the close of the season)?

a. 5

b. 6

c. 7

d. 9

14. Which of the Rangers didn't hit a homer in the World Series of 2010? World Series?

a. Nelson Cruz

b. Ian Kinsler

c. Mitch Moreland

d. Josh Hamilton

15. Which Rangers did not hit a homer in the 11th World Series?

a.Elvis Andrus

b.Adrian Beltre

c.Mike Napoli

d.Michael Young

16. The Texas Rangers won their first American League West Division Championship Title in the year 1995.

a.True

b.False

17. What side played The Texas Rangers play in the 2012 American League Wild Card game?

a.New York Yankees

b.Kansas City Royals

c.Detroit Tigers

d.Baltimore Orioles

18. What was the result of Game 3 in 2010's World Series? 2010 World Series?

a.Rangers 2 Giants 4

b.Rangers 4. Giants 2

c.Rangers 7 Giants 11

d.Rangers Giants 7, Giants 7

19. What was the result of Game 4 in 2011's World Series? 2011 World Series?

a.Rangers 4 Cardinals 0

b.Rangers 1, Cardinals 4

c.Rangers 3. Cardinals 2

d.Rangers 2 Cardinals 3

20. Which Ranger was not a part in BOTH both the World Series of 2011? World Series?

a.Nelson Cruz

b.Mitch Moreland

c.Jeff Francoeur

d. Josh Hamilton

Quiz Answers

1. A - 0

2. B - 2

3. C - San Francisco Giants

4. A - St. Louis Cardinals

5. D - 2012

6. D - 7

7. A - True

8. B - Ron Washington

9. B - 5

10. C - Cliff Lee

11. A - C.J. Wilson

12. B - False Josh Hamilton was named ALCS MVP in 2010.

13. C - 7

14. B - Ian Kinsler

15. A - Elvis Andrus

16. B - False. The team won their first championship in the year 1996.

17. D - Baltimore Orioles

18. B - Rangers 4, Giants 2

19. A - Rangers 4, Cardinals 0

20. C C Jeff Francoeur (He only played in the 2010 World Series.)

Did You Know?

1. The Texas Rangers are one of five MLB teams who have participated during the World Series but have never had a win. The remaining four teams include those of the San Diego Padres, the Colorado Rockies, the Tampa Bay Rays and the Milwaukee Brewers. It is the Seattle Mariners, the Rangers' AL West Division foe is the sole team that has not been in the World Series (as of the conclusion of the 2019 season).

2. The names of the players who have been put on the shelf to the Rangers, Nolan Ryan won one World Series with the New York Mets in 1969. Ivan "Pudge" Rodriguez won one World Series with the Florida Marlins in 2003. Michael Young and Adrian Beltre did not win one World Series.

3. Nelson Cruz had the most bats with the Rangers during the 2009 World Series, with 20. Adrian Beltre had the most bats with the Rangers during 2011, the World Series, with 30.

4. Neftali Feliz made one save during the World Series of 2010 and recorded one save in the World Series and two saves during the 2011 World Series.

Chapter 19: Heated Rivalries

Quiz Time!

1. Which team doesn't play within the American League West with the Rangers?

a. Oakland A's

b. Los Angeles Dodgers

c. Seattle Mariners

d. Houston Astros

2. The Houston Astros and Texas Rangers never played each other in the MLB postseason.

a. True

b. False

3. The Texas Rangers play the Houston Astros What is the game referred to?

a. Texas Series

b. Gold Boot Series

c. Cowboy Series

d.Lone Star Series

4. In the days before when the Houston Astros moved to the American League West, a trophy was presented to the winning team of the league's interleague Lone Star Series. What did the title of this trophy?

a.The Lone Star

b.The Silver Boot

c.The Gold Cowboy Hat

d.The Silver Horse

5. What was the date of the first event of the Lone Star Series?

a.June 8, 1999

b.September 6, 2001

c.June 8, 2001

d.September 6, 1999

6. The Rangers are yet to win the World Series championship as of at the conclusion of the

season. What number of World Series titles do the Astros own?

a. 0

b. 1

c. 2

d. 3

7. The Rangers as well as the Houston Astros shared the Astrodome during a brief time, that is the main reason in their rivalry.

a. True

b. False

8. Which player below have NOT played with BOTH those teams, the Texas Rangers AND the Houston Astros?

a. Ivan Rodriguez

b. Cliff Lee

c. C.J. Nitkowski

d. Robinson Chirinos

9. What was the size of used to receive the Silver Boot trophy from Houston Astros in addition to Texas Rangers' interleague play?

a.12

b.13

c.14

d.15

10. In the final days of the 2019 season what is the number of games that have been played in both the Houston Astros and Texas Rangers?

a.105

b.205

c.305

d.405

11. Present Texas Rangers manager Chris Woodward was a player with who was the American League West rival during his career when he was an infielder?

a.Seattle Mariners

b.Los Angeles Angels from Anaheim

c.Houston Astros

d.Oakland A's

12. The Texas Rangers have NEVER faced the American League West team in the playoffs.

a.True

b.False

13. Which one of these players didn't play in BOTH those of the Texas Rangers AND the Los Angeles Angels of Anaheim?

a.Sandy Alomar

b.Bobby Bonds

c.Bert Campaneris

d.Shin-Soo Choo

14. Which one of these players have NOT played with BOTH those of the Texas Rangers AND the Seattle Mariners?

a. Adrian Beltre

b. Nelson Cruz

c. Harold Baines

d. Jeff Burroughs

15. Which one of the below players have NOT played for BOTH those of the Texas Rangers AND the Oakland A's?

a. Prince Fielder

b. Jose Canseco

c. Bartolo Colon

d. Bert Campaneris

16. The Houston Astros defeated the Rangers on March 31, 2013 during their debut game in the American League West Division.

a. True

b. False

17. The San Francisco Giants defeated the Rangers in the 2010 World Series. What

number of World Series championships do the Giants own?

a. 3

b. 6

c. 8

d. 10

18. The St. Louis Cardinals defeated the Rangers in the 2011 World Series. What number of World Series championships do the Cardinals own?

a. 9

b. 11

c. 12

d. 17

19. Nolan Ryan is the only player in MLB history to win "the" DHL Hometown Hero of both clubs (both the Rangers as well as the Astros).

Chapter 20: The Awards Section

Quiz Time!

1. Who is the one Ranger ever to have won a Hank Aaron Award? (He received three.)

a. Adrian Beltre

b. Vladimir Guerrero

c. Alex Rodriguez

d. Josh Hamilton

2. None of the Rangers management has been awarded this award. American League Manager of the Year Award.

a. True

b. False

3. Who's the only Rangers pitcher to have won the Gold Glove? (He has won four.)

a. Nolan Ryan

b. Kenny Rogers

c. Fergie Jenkins

d.Gaylord Perry

4. Which player most recently took home most recently the AL Rookie of the Year Award (as at the close of the season)?

a.Mike Hargrove

b.Michael Young

c.Jurickson Profar

d.Neftali Feliz

5. What number of Gold Glove Awards did Ivan Rodriguez get during his time as a player for the Rangers?

a.10

b.2

c.6

d.12

6. Which Ranger won the 2010 Home Run Derby?

a.Vladimir Guerrero

b. Nelson Cruz

c. Michael Young

d. Josh Hamilton

7. There is no Rangers players have ever been awarded an award like the Cy Young Award.

a. True

b. False

8. Which Rangers player won the title of DHL Hometown Hero? (Voted from MLB fans as being the most remarkable player in the history of the franchise.)

a. Michael Young

b. Nolan Ryan

c. Ivan Rodriguez

d. Elvis Andrus

9. Which Rangers player took home the 2004 All-Star Game MVP Award?

a. Michael Young

b. Adrian Gonzalez

c. Alfonso Soriano

d. Mark Teixeira

10. Who was the sole Rangers player to ever win the Rawlings Platinum Gold Glove?

a. Adrian Beltre

b. Ivan Rodriguez

c. Ian Kinsler

d. Mitch Moreland

11. Which Ranger won the 1974 NL MVP Award?

a. Fergie Jenkins

b. Mike Hargrove

c. Dave Nelson

d. Jeff Burroughs

Chapter 21: The American Dream City

Quiz Time!

1. In Globe Life Park, home of the Texas Rangers, the Boomstick is a 2 foot all-beef hot dog that is smothered with Chili, Nacho Cheese jalapenos, caramelized onions and jalapenos over an immense potato bun. It weighs at just 3 pounds. What's the cost of it cost? Boomstick cost (as of)?

a.$15

b.$22

c.$26

d.$32

2. Dot races and ballpark nachos were invented in Arlington Stadium, former home of the Texas Rangers.

a.True

b.False

3. The name was "Vegas before Vegas," which was the secret gambling center in Arlington between the 1930s and 1920s?

a.Top O Mountain Terrace

b.Top O World Terrace

c.Top O Hill Terrace

d.Top O Tree Terrace

4. Which automaker has opened an assembly facility in Arlington in the year 1954?

a.Volkswagen

b.Chevrolet

c.Ford

d.General Motors

5. The shoe's founder brand was born in and was a child in Arlington?

a.Converse

b.TOMS

c.Vans

d.Birkenstock

6. Arlington has more than 380,000 residents, which makes Arlington the largest urban area of the United States by population.

a.30th

b.40th

c.50th

d.60th

7. Arlington is home to American Mensa.

a.True

b.False

8. What's the name of the NFL team currently calling Arlington the home of its team?

a.Dallas Dodgers

b.Dallas Cowboys

c.Dallas Raiders

d. Dallas Mavericks

9. What's the name for the NBA team that is closest to Arlington?

a. Dallas Cowboys

b. Dallas Knicks

c. Dallas Warriors

d. Dallas Mavericks

10. Which year was the city of Arlington founded?

a. 1866

b. 1876

c. 1886

d. 1896

11. Arlington is the home of Six Flags over Texas AND Six Flags _____.

Chapter 22: Young At Heart

Quiz Time!

1. In which country was Michael Young born?

a. Pomona, California

b. Covina, California

c. Anaheim, California

d. Temecula, California

2. Michael Young is currently special as the assistant to the general manager of the Rangers.

a. True

b. False

3. Michael Young played for three teams in the course of his MLB professional career. Which team did he do not played for?

a. Seattle Mariners

b. Texas Rangers

c. Los Angeles Dodgers

d. Philadelphia Phillies

4. Which year was the year that Michael Young born?

a. 1971

b. 1973

c. 1975

d. 1976

5. In what year was the Michael Young's number 10 removed from the Texas Rangers?

a. 2016

b. 2017

c. 2019

d. They are not been able to retire his number.

6. In the 25th Round in the 1994 MLB Draft, Michael Young was chosen by _____, but he did not make the decision to sign. Michael Young was again drafted during the 5th round of 1997's MLB Draft by the _____.

a. Baltimore Orioles, Toronto Blue Jays

b. Toronto Blue Jays, Baltimore Orioles

c. Texas Rangers, Toronto Blue Jays

d. Toronto Blue Jays, Texas Rangers

7. Michael Young is in the National Baseball Hall of Fame.

a. True

b. False

8. Which college Did Michael Young attend college?

a. University of California Irvine Irvine

b. San Diego State University

c. Pepperdine University

d. University of California Santa Barbara Santa Barbara

9. In which school was the place that Michael Young attend high school?

a.Bishop amat memorial high school

b.San Gabriel High School

c.Gabrielino High School

d.South El Monte High School

10. Michael Young launched his own charity in the year 2011. The purpose of the charity is to become "a charity which supports the involvement of children's health in all areas: physical, social, mental, and educational." What's the title of his organization?

a.The Michael Young Foundation

b.Young Foundation

c.Michael Young Family Foundation

d.Young Family Foundation

www.ingramcontent.com/pod-product-compliance
Lightning Source LLC
Chambersburg PA
CBHW071447080526
44587CB00014B/2025